## Discovering
## Cultures

# Greece

## Sharon Gordon

**B**ENCHMARK **B**OOKS

MARSHALL CAVENDISH
NEW YORK

With thanks to Dr. George S. Yiangou, Research Fellow, Institute for the Study of Europe, Columbia University, for the careful review of this manuscript.

Benchmark Books
Marshall Cavendish
99 White Plains Road
Tarrytown, New York 10591-9001
www.marshallcavendish.com

Library of Congress Cataloging-in-Publication Data
Gordon, Sharon.
Greece / by Sharon Gordon.
p. cm. — (Discovering cultures)
Includes bibliographical references and index.
Summary: An introduction to the history, geography, language, schools, and social life and customs of Greece.
ISBN 0-7614-1718-4
1. Greece—Juvenile literature. [1. Greece.] I. Title. II. Series.
DF717.G65 2003
949.5—dc21                        2003008130

Photo Research by Candlepants Incorporated

Cover Photo: Charles O'Rear / *Corbis*

The photographs in this book are used by permission and through the courtesy of; *Corbis*: Charles & Josette Lenars, 1; Jon Hicks, 4; Wolfgang Kaehler, 6; Larry Lee, 7, 10, 42 (lower right); David Ball, 8; Gianni Dagli Orti, 11; Gail Mooney, 13, 17, 19, 22, 31, 35; Amet Jean Pierre/Sigma, 18; Roger Wood, 20-21; Gian Berto Vanni, 30; Sandro Vannini, 36, 42 (top left); AFP, 38. *Robert Fried/ Robert Fried Photography.com*: 9, 15, 16, 43 (middle), back cover. *Eugene G. Schulz*: 12. *Randa Bishop Photography LLC*: 14, 24, 25, 34. *Trip-Art Directors*: B. Turner, 26; Peter Robinson, 32; H. Rogers, 37. *Getty Images*: 29 (left), 43 (left), 44 (lower left); Mike Hewitt, 28; Grazia Neri, 29 (right); Hulton-Archive, 44 (top right), 45.

Cover: *The Parthenon*; Title page: *Greek woman in traditional dress*

Map and illustrations by Ian Warpole
Book design by Virginia Pope

Printed in China
1  3  5  6  4  2

# Turn the Pages...

# Where in the World Is Greece?

Greece is a warm, sunny country in southeastern Europe. It is at the bottom of the Balkan Peninsula. To the north are Albania, Bulgaria, and the Former Yugoslav Republic of Macedonia (F.Y.R.O.M.). Turkey and the Aegean Sea are to the east. The Ionian Sea is to the west. Both seas are part of the larger Mediterranean Sea.

Greece is a little smaller than the state of Alabama. No town is more than 60 miles (96 kilometers) from the sea. In addition to the mainland, Greece has more than

*This Greek town enjoys great views of the sea.*

# Map of Greece

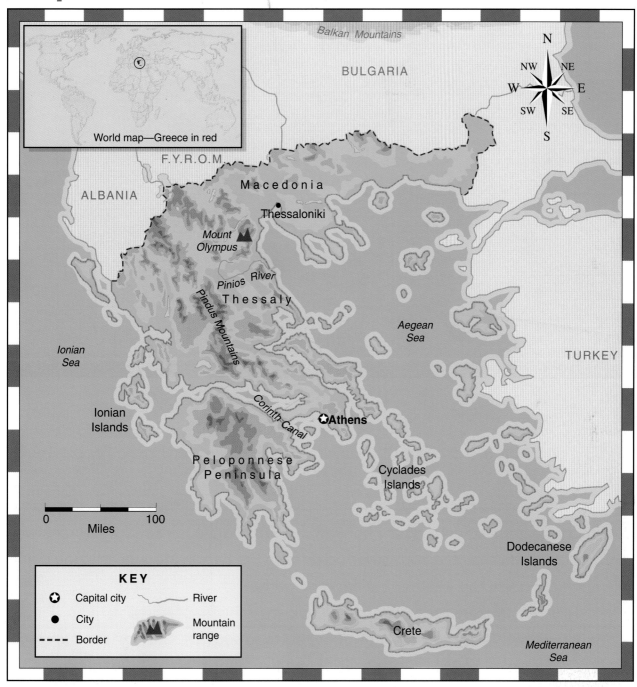

World map—Greece in red

Balkan Mountains

BULGARIA

F.Y.R.O.M.

ALBANIA

Macedonia

● Thessaloniki

Mount Olympus

Pinios River

Thessaly

Pindus Mountains

Ionian Sea

Aegean Sea

TURKEY

Ionian Islands

Corinth Canal

✪ Athens

Peloponnese Peninsula

Cyclades Islands

Dodecanese Islands

Crete

Mediterranean Sea

N
NW   NE
W         E
SW   SE
S

0        100
Miles

**KEY**

✪  Capital city          River

●  City                      Mountain range

- - -  Border

*A sunny grove of olive trees*

2,000 islands. Crete is the largest. Many of the islands are very small. People live on only 170 of them.

Greece enjoys about 250 days of sunshine every year. The climate is similar to southern California. Summers are hot and dry. Winters are mild and wet. In the winter, an icy wind called the bora drops down from the Balkan Mountains in the north. In spring and fall, the weather is pleasantly warm.

Hills or mountains cover more than two-thirds of Greece. The Pindus Mountains divide the country in two from north to south. The land has a rocky soil. The rocks make it hard for farmers to grow their crops. Many farmers grow olive trees, which do well, even in poor soil. In early winter, the farmers shake the trees. The ripe olives fall into nets on the ground. Then they are collected and made into olive oil.

Macedonia is a region in northern Greece. It has wide, flat land for farming corn, cotton, rice, and grapes. The grapes are made into wine. Thessaloniki is the capital of Macedonia and the second largest city in Greece. It is also an important seaport.

Thessaly is in central Greece. Wheat and cotton are grown here. The Pinios River cuts Thessaly in two. It is surrounded by tall mountain peaks. Greece's highest peak is Mount Olympus. It is 9,570 feet (2,917 meters) high. According to Greek *mythology*, the twelve Olympian gods and goddesses lived on the top of the mount. Zeus was the king of all the gods.

Athens is the capital of Greece and its largest city. It was once the center of Greek culture and trade. Today,

*Athens is the capital of Greece.*

Athens is still an important international city. People and cars jam the streets. Modern buildings have been built alongside the ancient *ruins*.

The Peloponnese Peninsula is in the south. It is not a true *peninsula* anymore because the Corinth Canal was built across it in the 1880s. Now it is more like an island, surrounded by water on all sides. The canal allows ships to sail through the peninsula. This is much easier and quicker than sailing around it.

*Boats on the Corinth Canal*

8

# The Acropolis

In the center of Athens stands a large, flattopped hill called the Acropolis. This is Greece's most famous archaeological site. Thousands of people visit the Acropolis each year. They come to see what is left of the amazing stone buildings that were built thousands of years ago. The ruins of a white marble temple called the Parthenon still stand. It was built in 432 B.C. It was dedicated to the goddess Athena. The Acropolis can be seen from any spot in Athens. The law does not allow people to put up buildings that block the view.

# What Makes Greece Greek?

Thousands of years of history make Greece Greek. It is a nation proud of its past and present. The ancient Greeks were famous for their *architecture*. They built beautiful buildings with large columns. They made huge marble statues of their leaders.

The ancient Greeks were great philosophers. The word philosophy means "the love of knowledge." The Greek philosophers were the first to use science and reason to explain the things around them. Some of the most famous Greek philosophers

*Ancient Greek architecture*

were Plato, Socrates, and Aristotle.

Greece was the first *democracy*. In a democracy, the people vote for their leaders. The United States is also a democracy. In both countries, the people vote for their leaders. They are not ruled by a king or a queen.

Greek is the official language of Greece. Many words in English come from Greek. In fact, the word "alphabet" comes from the first two letters in the Greek language: *alpha* and *beta*.

A statue of the famous Greek philosopher, Plato

The Greek language helped spread the Christian religion. The books of the New Testament of the Bible were first written in Greek. Today, many pastors and priests still learn Greek.

Almost everyone in Greece belongs to the Greek Orthodox Church. There is an Orthodox church in every town and village. The Greek priests have long hair and beards. They wear black robes and black hats. They are respected in the community.

Greek families are very close. Family members take care of each other. Children and grandchildren care for old or sick parents and grandparents. Families

*A Greek Orthodox priest*

support poor relatives. It is unusual to see a homeless person in Greece.

Every Greek child has a *nonos*, or godparent. Godparents help children understand their religion. They make sure a child is happy and secure. According to Greek religious law, children of godparents cannot marry, even though they are not related. In the eyes of the church, they are brother and sister.

Until recently, many Greek families lived in the countryside in small communities. They stayed in the same community throughout their lives. Many started their own businesses. Parents, children, aunts, uncles,

*Greek children are cared for by many adults.*

13

*A Greek father and his sons*

and even cousins worked together. These businesses were passed down through the families. Today, many of Greece's small modern shipping companies are family-owned businesses.

# Traditional Greek Clothing

Festivals and parades are often held in Greece. They celebrate important national and religious holidays. People wear traditional clothes to perform Greek folk dances. Boys wear a cotton skirt called the *foustanela* along with a long-sleeved shirt and stockings. It is believed that the skirts helped the men run fast because their legs were free. Girls' costumes are different from one part of Greece to another. Some have long colorful skirts with velvet jackets. Others wear white dresses with a velvet vest, an embroidered apron, a scarf, and a chain with coins. Both boys and girls wear shoes with fuzzy pom-poms called *tsarouhia*.

# Living in Greece

This woman enjoys some fresh air on her patio.

Greeks love to be outdoors. Their homes are places to eat, dress, and sleep. But for everything else, they head outside. On warm evenings, families walk through the streets to meet their friends. Many houses and apartments have a patio or balcony where people sit and relax. In the summer, vines cover these areas with shade. This outdoor living space also is used to grow plants, herbs, and flowers.

Although they have supermarkets, many Greeks still shop at small stores and outdoor markets. They like to pick up fresh bread and baked goods each day. Fresh vegetables, cheese, fish, and meats are available at local markets. Open booths called kiosks are popular places to buy small items like

newspapers, stamps, and cards. In some villages, street vendors in open trucks travel from town to town. They carry fruits, vegetables, and meats through the streets for people to buy.

Lamb is the most common meat in Greece. With seas all around, fish is also popular. So is chicken. Feta cheese, made from goat's milk, is the national cheese. It is enjoyed on Greek salads. Pita bread is often stuffed with meat and vegetables for a sandwich. Homegrown fruit with yogurt makes a perfect dessert.

The day begins with a very light breakfast. For most Greeks, lunch is the largest meal. Then they rest in the

*Fresh fruits and vegetables at an outdoor market*

*A busy street in Athens*

heat of the day. In the cool evenings, people go out to *tavernas*, or restaurants, to socialize with friends. They sing and dance to exciting Greek music.

City life is busy and crowded. One-third of Greeks live in or around Athens. Athens has many buildings. There are few places for parks and recreation. Smog

*Relaxing at a cafe*

and pollution are problems in the city. Many people hope that Athens' subway train will help reduce pollution. It is fast and does not cost much to ride.

Many Greeks live in the countryside in small farming or fishing villages. They live in homes built of stone or *stucco*. Homes in the south and on the

islands are painted white. This helps reflect the sun and keep the houses cool. Villagers gather at the *kafenion* (coffeehouse) to talk about their work or families. They sip strong Greek coffee called *kafedaki*.

Greeks can also visit friends on-line at an Internet cafe. People who do not have computers in their own homes can pay to use public computers. Internet cafes are also popular with travelers. They can log on to the Internet to send e-mails or pay their bills on-line. Some Internet cafes serve food and drink, too.

Buses are widely used for transportation around Greece. Small boats or ferries take people between the mainland and the islands. Because of the mountains, roads are often steep and winding. Some people living on the islands still get around in horse-drawn carriages instead of cars. Farmers use donkeys and mules

*White stone houses are built to stay cool in the hot sun.*

*Ferries take people from island to island.*

to travel on streets that are too narrow for cars or carriages. Children walk or ride their bikes.

Tourism is important to Greece. Millions of people visit the country each year. The ruins in Athens and the Greek islands are very popular. Island shops carry colorful clothes and pottery. Tourists can buy beautiful Greek *embroidery* and woven goods.

# Let's Eat!
## Feta Cheese and Spinach Salad

This Greek salad is easy to make. Ask an adult to help you prepare this recipe.

**Ingredients:**

2 cups raw spinach

1/4 cup cooked white rice

1 hard-boiled egg, cut in quarters

1 small cucumber, diced

1 small sweet red pimiento,
chopped in 1/4 inch pieces

1 1/2 ounces crumbled Feta cheese

2 tablespoons vinegar dressing

4 Greek olives

Wash your hands. Mix the spinach with the rice, egg, pimiento, cucumber, and Feta cheese. Add dressing and mix lightly. Sprinkle with Greek olives. Serves two.

# School Days

Education is important in Greece. More than 95 percent of Greeks can read and write. Students work very hard. Their parents expect them to do well in school. The success of the children makes the whole family proud.

All children must go to school from ages six to fifteen. From six to twelve, they attend primary school. They go from grades A to F instead of first through sixth. Secondary school is divided into Gymnasium and Lyceum. From ages twelve to fifteen students go to the Gymnasium. From fifteen to eighteen they go to the Lyceum.

Every teacher has about twenty-five students. But in small villages and on the islands, there might be only one school and not many teachers. A classroom might be mixed with children of all ages. The teacher has to teach to all the levels.

Education in Greece is free and students can keep their textbooks at the end

*Greek students listen in class.*

*Children at work on the blackboard*

of each year. Preschool classes for children ages three to five are also free. Most children go to public schools, even the rich children. They do not wear uniforms to school.

For teachers, the school year begins on September 1 and it ends on June 21. The children start school on a Monday in mid-September and are finished by mid-June. They get two weeks off for Christmas and Easter. School begins at 8:30 A.M. Children study geography, math, history, and religion. They also learn to read and write Greek. Students work all morning and go home in the early afternoon for lunch.

Many students take private lessons in the afternoon in subjects not covered at school. They study music, languages, or sports. Older students have private lessons to help prepare for their university exams. After the private lessons are over, students do their homework. Younger children help with household chores. Older

*The University of Athens*

children might have jobs in the family business or farm. They bring extra money into their homes. When all the work is done, it is finally time to go out and play!

Today, more Greek families want their children to attend a university. Poorer families hope that an education will help their children get good jobs. Farmers hope their children will not have to work hard in the fields like they did. But not everyone who wants to go to college can get in. There are too many students and not enough universities.

Greece has sixteen universities. The University of Athens and the Aristotelian University in Thessaloniki are the largest. There are special schools for *archaeology* and other sciences. Students compete to get in by taking difficult tests. Those who cannot get into Greek universities often go to colleges in Europe and the United States. Outside the country, there are more universities and more subjects to study.

# Secret Schools

For four hundred years, the Ottoman Turks ruled over Greece. It is believed that the Turks did not allow the Greeks to study the Greek language. Greeks could not pass on their culture to their children. The Greek Orthodox Church began to set up *krypho scholio* (secret schools) in monasteries throughout the country. Monks or priests taught children about their culture in these schools. They often met at night, when children were thought to be sleeping. The Orthodox Church kept the Greek language and traditions alive during this time. This is one reason why the cross in the Greek flag is so important to the Greek people.

# Just for Fun

Lighting the Olympic torch

"**L**et the games begin!" The Olympic games began in Greece in 776 B.C. Greek athletes gathered in the valley of Olympia. They competed in various sports to honor the god Zeus. The games were a part of Greek religion. The original Olympic games were wrestling, jumping, and *chariot* racing. Modern Olympic games still begin at Olympia, Greece, with the lighting of the Olympic flame. The torch is then carried by runners or by plane to the host city. Greeks were thrilled when Athens was chosen to host the 2004 Olympic Games.

Soccer is the Greek national sport. It is called *podosphero* in Greece. Children learn how to play when they are very young. The Greek national

*Soccer stars*

*The Acropolis Rally*

soccer team competes with countries from around the world. Often, the team is good enough to play in the World Cup. Basketball is as popular as soccer. Volleyball is another favorite sport.

Car-racing fans come to the Acropolis Rally in June every year. It is part of the World Rally Championship. The Acropolis Rally is one of the oldest and toughest road rallies. Drivers must face rough roads with huge rocks that can rip up their tires or damage their cars.

The Pindus Mountains and the Peloponnese hills are popular with nature lovers. Both Greeks and tourists enjoy hiking along the many trails on Greece's mainland. But when the snow comes, these same mountains are filled with skiers. The season runs from December through March. But some of Greece's steepest mountains are covered with snow much later. In late spring, it is possible to ski in the morning and swim in the warm sea in the afternoon.

In Greek cities and towns, adults may sit down to enjoy a favorite board game, like backgammon. Others gather at a cafe to discuss politics. Teenagers walk to the theater to see a movie with their friends. Parks fill up with families and children who want to enjoy the weather. Under a shady tree, a young poet, writer, or artist may be at work.

Greek children enjoy flying kites in the beautiful weather. They like to ride their bikes and play games with their friends. Like American children, they play hide-and-seek, hopscotch, leapfrog, and kickball. Greek children also like to play a game of marbles called Trigonaki. It is played with one big marble called mom and ten small marbles called the kids. It is not a good idea to hit your mom with your marble!

Greek arts and crafts have been around for thousands of years. Many pieces of pottery that have been discovered tell us what life was like in ancient Greece. The artwork on old vases and pots tells us about religion, favorite games, and even the kinds of pets that were kept. Today, many Greeks still enjoy the art of

*Ancient statue of a Greek goddess*

*Windsurfers enjoy the beautiful blue seas.*

pottery. Perhaps in the future people will study the pots and vases of today to learn what Greek life was like in the twenty-first century!

Since the beautiful sea is all around, many families head to the beaches on the weekends. Children learn to swim at a very young age. If a family gets tired of swimming, they can switch to fishing or snorkeling. Water sports, such as windsurfing, sailing, and waterskiing, are also popular.

Greece has many wonderful museums that show its rich history. These are favorite places for both Greeks and tourists to visit. The National Archaeological

*The National Archaeological Museum of Athens*

Museum of Athens has a special collection of Greek sculpture and art. The Acropolis Museum has treasures that have been discovered right on the famous hill. Almost all of the Greek islands also have their own museums filled with local folk art.

# Abarisa

Greek children have played this simple outdoor game for many years. The children divide into two teams. Each team chooses a tree or other area as their "home," or *abarisa*. The object is for one team to take over the other team's home. When a child leaves his home, he calls out "Abarisa!" A member of the other team tries to catch the child before he gets to the other team's home. If the child is caught, he or she must go to jail. The team can free the jailed player by saying "Xele." The children continue to leave their homes. They try to get to the other team's home without getting caught. The first team to successfully reach the other team's home and call "Abarisa!" wins the game.

# Let's Celebrate!

Only children celebrate their birthdays in Greece. Name days are more important in Greece than birthdays. Often, people are named after a Greek Orthodox saint. They celebrate their name day on that saint's feast day. People celebrating a name day might receive a call from friends who say, "Chronia polla (I hope you have many happy years)!" Visitors may bring them a box of chocolates or flowers. Some children up to the age of twelve have parties on their name days and their birthdays!

*Birthday smiles*

*Playing the bouzouki*

There are Greek festivals all year long. Most of them include lively music, singing, and dancing. Greeks have always loved music. In fact the word "music" comes from the Nine Muses of ancient Greece. Greek musicians play traditional wind instruments like the *zourna*. The *bouzouki* looks like a plump, round guitar. Dancers in costumes perform Greek folk dances. Guests toast each other by clinking their glasses and saying, "Yiassas (Your health)!"

*An Easter procession*

The Skyros Carnival is held just before the season of Lent. It has some unusual traditions. Young men wear goat masks, hairy jackets, and dozens of copper goat bells. They stroll around town, ringing their bells. One man dresses up as a bride who also wears a goat mask. What a couple!

*Greek Easter bread*

Pascha (Easter) is the most important religious celebration. Greek Orthodox ceremonies remember the suffering and death of Jesus Christ. In many villages, people walk through the center of town with candles on Good Friday. Church services are held late on Saturday night. At midnight, the priest lights a candle and cries, "Christos anesti (Christ is risen)!" The church bells ring as people go into the streets with flickering candles. Fireworks light the dark skies. The next day, on Easter Sunday, families celebrate with a feast of roasted lamb.

Christmas is a quieter holiday in Greece than in the United States. Just recently, people in big cities have begun to put up Christmas trees. Many Greeks give up eating certain foods in the weeks before Christmas. On Christmas Day, they look forward to a great feast. The traditional meal is a roast pig, lamb, or goat.

*Lighting a Christmas tree*

Honey-dipped cookies called *melomakarona* are favorite Greek Christmas cookies. A round loaf of Christopsomo (Christ bread) is decorated with a cross. Sometimes, the family adds little shapes to show their jobs, like a fish for a fisherman. They make a toast and say, "Kala Christouyenna (Merry Christmas)!"

# Kallikantzari

The days between Christmas and the Epiphany on January 6 are called the Twelve Days of Christmas. During this time, the Greeks must deal with the pesky Kallikantzari (kali-KANZ-ah-ree). Unlike Santa's helpful elves, these little troublemakers play tricks on people for twelve days. Some people say the Kallikantzari look like wolves or monkeys. Others describe them as mean fairies who wear wooden or iron boots for kicking people! Are they real or imaginary? To be safe, Greeks keep fires burning in their fireplaces so the Kallikantzari cannot enter their homes. Strong herbs are hung by the fireplace to keep these evil spirits away. On the Epiphany, a local priest performs the "Blessing of the Waters." Then it is believed the Kallikantzari are finally chased away—until next year!

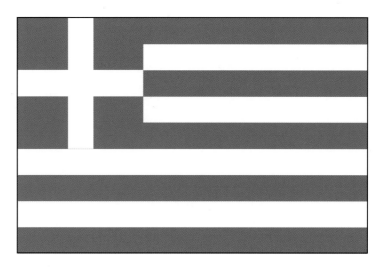

The Greek flag is blue and white. It has five blue stripes and four white stripes. Blue stands for the blue skies and seas of Greece. The white stands for the pure fight of freedom. The Christian cross in the top left corner is from the Greek Orthodox Church.

Greece is a member of the European Union (EU). In January 2002, Greece and eleven other states within the EU began to use the same currency, or money. This currency is called the euro. Euro coins share common European designs on the front, but the designs on the back of the coins change from nation to nation. Euro banknotes, or paper money, are the same in all twelve nations.

# Count in Greek

| English | Greek | Say it like this: |
|---------|-------|-------------------|
| one | ena | eh-nah |
| two | dio | thee-oh |
| three | tria | tree-ah |
| four | tesera | tes-eh-rah |
| five | pente | pen-deh |
| six | exi | ex-see |
| seven | efta | ef-tah |
| eight | okto | ock-toh |
| nine | enia | en-nea |
| ten | deka | theh-ka |

# Glossary

**archaeology** (ar-kee-OL-uh-jee)   The study of the way people lived a long time ago.

**architecture** (AR-ki-tek-chur)   A particular style or way of building.

**chariot** (CHAR-ee-uht)   A vehicle with two wheels that is pulled by horses.

**democracy**   A government in which the people vote for their leaders.

**embroidery** (em-BROY-duh-ree)   Designs that are sewn on cloth with thread.

**Muses** (MYOOZ-es)   Greek goddesses who guided the works of song and poetry.

**mythology**   Stories that tell how things came to be.

**peninsula**   A piece of land that is surrounded by water on three sides.

**ruins** (ROO-ins)   The remains of an old building that has fallen down over the years.

**stucco**   A mixture of cement and sand used to cover the outside of a building.

# Fast Facts

Greece is a little smaller than the state of Alabama.

In addition to the mainland, Greece has more than 2,000 islands. Crete is the largest.

Macedonia
Thessaloniki
Mount Olympus
Pinios River
Thessaly
Pindus Mountains
Corinth Canal
Ionian Islands
Athens
Peloponnese Peninsula
Cyclades Islands
Dodecanese Islands
Crete

Greece was the first democracy. In a democracy, the people vote for their leaders.

Athens is the capital of Greece and its largest city. One-third of Greeks live in or around Athens.

The Greek flag is blue and white. It has five blue stripes and four white stripes. The blue stands for the blue skies and seas of Greece. The white stands for the pure fight of freedom. The Christian cross is from the Greek Orthodox Church.

Greece's highest peak is Mount Olympus. It is 9,570 feet (2,917 m) high.

In 2003, 98 percent of Greeks were Greek Orthodox, 1.3 percent were Muslim, and 0.7 percent followed other religions.

Greece is a member of the European Union (EU). In January 2002, Greece and eleven other states within the EU began to use the same currency, or money. This currency is called the euro.

The Olympic games began in Greece in 776 B.C.

In the center of Athens stands a large, flattopped hill called the Acropolis. The ruins of a white marble temple called the Parthenon still stand on the Acropolis. It was built in 432 B.C.

Soccer is the Greek national sport. It is called podosphero in Greece.

As of July 2002, 10,645,343 people lived in Greece.

# Proud to Be Greek

## Maria Callas (1923–1977)

Maria's real name was Cecilia Sophia Anna Maria Kalogeropoulos. She was born to Greek immigrants in New York City. She moved to Greece with her mother and sister in 1937 after her parents separated. She began to study opera with the well-known Elvira de Hidalgo at the National Conservatory in Athens. After three years of study, she appeared with the Lyric Theatre Company in Athens at the age of seventeen. She became known for her rich voice and her ability to make her characters come to life. She came to New York and performed with the Metropolitan Opera in 1956. Maria died in Paris in 1977. Her ashes were scattered in the Aegean Sea.

## Pyrros Dimas (1971–    )

Three-time Olympic gold medalist Pyrros Dimas was born in Albania to Greek parents. Before he began lifting weights, Dimas lifted concrete blocks for his job in construction. He joined a weightlifting club and started to train seriously. In 1991, he moved to Greece. He took everyone by surprise by winning the gold medal in Barcelona in 1992. On his return to Greece, he was given a hero's welcome. He won a second gold medal in Atlanta in 1996. He was honored along with other Greek gold medalists at the Temple of Zeus. He won his third gold medal in Sydney, Australia in 2000. Dimas is so strong, he can lift twice his own weight.

## Aristotelis "Telly" Savalas (1924–1994)

Most people remember Telly Savalas as the lollipop-sucking detective named Kojak. His hit television series of the 1970s made Savalas a household name. Before then he had been an announcer for the Greek Voice of America. He had also been a producer for ABC News. His parents immigrated to New York from Greece. During the Depression, Savalas and his brother sold newspapers and started a shoeshine business to help earn money for their family. Savalas loved his homeland of Greece and made many films about it. He died in New York in 1994. His godchild is another well-known television star, Jennifer Aniston.

# Find Out More

## Books

*Enchantment of the World: Greece* by Ann Heinrichs. Children's Press, Danbury, CT, 2002.

*Countries of the World: Greece* by Yeoh Hong Nam. Gareth Stevens Publishing, Milwaukee, WI, 1999.

*Modern Nations of the World: Greece* by Don Nardo. Lucent Books, San Diego, CA, 2000.

*A True Book: Greece* by Christine & David Peterson. Children's Press, Danbury, CT, 2001.

*Greece* by Julia Waterlow. The Bookwright Press, New York, 1992.

## Web Sites

Go to **www.ancientgreece.com** to find out more about Greek history, mythology, art, and architecture.

Visit the Embassy of Greece in Washington, D.C. on-line at **www.greekembassy.org**.

## Video

*Greece: Athens, the Peloponnese, and the Greek Islands*, 52 minutes. Travel Video Cyberstore, 1999.

# Index

Page numbers for illustrations are in **boldface.**

# About the Author

Sharon Gordon has written many nature and science books for young children. She has worked as an advertising copywriter and a book club editor. She is writing other books for the *Discovering Cultures* series. Sharon and her husband Bruce have three teenage children, Douglas, Katie, and Laura, and one spoiled pooch, Samantha. They live in Midland Park, New Jersey. The family especially enjoys traveling to the Outer Banks of North Carolina. After she puts her three children through college, Sharon hopes to visit the many exciting places she has come to love through her writing and research.